Tales
of a
ROAD
WARRIOR

Tales
of a
ROAD
WARRIOR

HARVEY STEELE

White Bear Publishing

I have tried to recreate events, locations, and conversations from my memories of them. In order to protect their privacy and maintain their anonymity, in many instances I have changed the names and identifying characteristics of individuals.

Cover Design & Illustrations: Guy Harvey
Copy Editing & Proofreading: Adria Carey Perez

ISBN-13: 979-8-9893475-2-0
Library of Congress Control Number: 2023919881
Second Edition – January 2024

Published by White Bear Publishing
Ramsey, MN
Printed in the United States of America

DEDICATION

This book is dedicated to my many travel companions over the years – family, friends, colleagues, and customers. Some are gone now – Scott Hunt, Joe Sczepanski, Rich White, Phil Lepofsky, Sergio Garue, Jerry Grady, Marty Siegel, Bob McKinley, and Laurel Crowe – but not forgotten.

I have frequently used fictional names in this book to protect the innocent – or guilty – as the case may be.

"Traveling – it leaves you speechless, then turns you into a storyteller."

Ibn Battuta

Table of Contents

Introduction

Over the past forty-plus years, I have had the opportunity to travel extensively for both business and pleasure. My modes of transportation have included cars, bus, train, boat, and airplanes of all varieties. In total, I estimate that I have traveled over four million miles, or about one hundred sixty times around the world.

My travels have taken me to:

- Forty-six US States, DC, Puerto Rico, and the US Virgin Islands
- Thirty-five foreign countries

This amount of travel has its high and low points.

Low Points:

- Lots of time sitting in the car, in airports, on airplanes, etc.
- The "opportunity" to experience the vagaries of travel

High Points:

- Exciting experiences seeing much of the world
- Learning about other people and cultures
- Having friends in many different places

Over the years I have collected many true travel stories. While most are humorous, others teach patience and understanding. I have related several of these stories to friends and family, and a frequent response is that you could not make this up and that I should write it all down.

My purpose for this book is to share these stories and hopefully give the reader a few laughs and perhaps some light lessons in patience and enjoying our cultural differences. I am sure my many fellow "road warriors" out there have had similar experiences.

Harvey Steele
2023

Holy Grappa!

There is considerable truth to the statement that you really get to know a person when you travel with them. I was lucky in that I had many opportunities to travel with coworkers and customers, forming great memories and lasting relationships.

Due to some product-related issues, I made an emergency trip with some engineers from one of the Big Three automakers to Italy. We spent several long days working on the problem with engineers and designers from my own company. Since we still had work to do, and people needed a break, we ended up staying in Italy for the weekend.

On Friday night, after the long work week, we all went out to dinner to blow off some steam. Besides wonderful food, we also had a fair amount of particularly good Italian wine. After dinner, I ordered everyone some grappa. Suffice it to say that grappa, which is a wine-based brandy containing 35-60% alcohol, packs a punch and is an acquired taste. All these years later and I still don't understand how anyone could enjoy drinking it.

The next morning, still suffering some of the effects of the wine and grappa, we set off for a day trip from Milan to Venice, about a two-hour drive. And what a pretty drive, as west of Venice you pass through wine country.

Northeastern Italy – Lombardy, the Veneto, Friuli, Trentino, and Alto Adige – is a major wine producing area, particularly for pinot grigio. From its footing in this region, pinot grigio grew to become the most popular white wine in all of Italy, and then the most popular imported white wine in the US.

So, here we are driving along, admiring the beautiful scenery, when one of the engineers, we'll call him Frank, says, "Hey, look at that!" and starts laughing. I look, and I see a man standing in a vineyard urinating on some grape vines.

I ask Frank, "What's so funny?"

Grappa
Taste the Terroir

He points at the urinating man. "He's peeing on the grapes!" With as straight a face as I can muster, I say, "Yes, he is." I can see that Frank is confused, so I ask him, "Do you remember the grappa we had last night?"

"Of course, how could I forget it, why?" So, I say in a serious tone, "Those are grappa grapes!"

Over thirty years later and I can still clearly picture the look on his face. To this day I am not sure if he knows that I was joking.

"A hangover is the wrath of grapes."

Dorothy Parker

Senso Unico

Part of my job involved routinely taking customers to visit our facilities in Italy for things like audits, contract negotiations, and design reviews.

On one such trip I was attending an audit along with a quality assurance engineer, Marty, and a buyer, Bill, from the customer. Audits can be quite boring if you are not intimately involved, as they dig through endless documentation.

After two days of the audit, we decided to go from the suburbs into downtown Milan for dinner. I had rented a car and agreed to drive the customers to dinner. My colleagues gave me directions (this is long before GPS in the car came on the scene), and we hit the road.

The best way to describe driving in downtown Milan is to visualize a map that looks a lot like a circular maze. So, I am driving along, making what I believe to be the correct turns, as I've driven downtown before, but it is taking us a while to find the restaurant.

Suddenly Marty starts yelling at me, "Stop, you're going in circles!"

"No, I'm not. I know where I'm going."

He insists that I do not, and he wasn't shy about telling me so, and says, "Yes, you are. We have passed the same street five or six times."

Now I am getting concerned and losing a little confidence, but I persist: "I know where we're going. What street do you think we've passed that many times?"

He points to a street sign and says, "That one!"

I look over. The sign says "Senso Unico."

"Marty, that is Italian for "One Way."

Trust me when I say that Bill never let Marty forget about it.

"Do not expect good direction from someone who has never made the journey."

Unknown

Where Were You on 9/11?

I was working as Sales Director for an electronics company in 2001. We were in the process of re-structuring our sales force and, as a result, I was interviewing various manufacturer's representative's firms in several locations around the country.

I left home in the Detroit suburbs early the morning of 9/11 for a flight to Indianapolis. All was well until about twenty minutes out of Detroit.

When it was obvious that the plane was making a 180-degree turn, everyone, including the flight attendants, looked around and wonder what's going on.

The pilot came on the intercom and said, "I'm sure you noticed that we turned around. I am following orders from air traffic control and will let you know why as soon as I know." He comes back on the air a few minutes later and says, "Well folks, we have been ordered back to Detroit and the reason I was given was 'national emergency.' You now know what I know, and we should be back on the ground in about twenty minutes."

Cell phones were not allowed to be used on planes and they did not have live TV at the time. We landed and there were no lights or sirens anywhere around the airport that we could see.

I was in first class and was one of the first off the plane, at which time I sprinted to the Northwest World Club at the end of the concourse. I arrived in time to see the re-runs of Flight 175 crashing into the World Trade Center. I stood in the World Club, along with many others, until we heard that Flight 73 had crashed into the Pentagon.

At that point, I left the airport and drove home. The rest of the day was spent in a fog of disbelief as we watched all the events unfold on TV.

Over the next couple of days business slowly started moving forward. By this time, I was upset, and we had major meetings scheduled in Phoenix. I decided that I would be on one of the first flights out of Detroit to Phoenix, which was on Sunday, September 16.

Many years later and everyone can tell you where they were and what they were doing on 9/11. Flying today is different than it used to be and always will be.

"Fate doesn't care about your plans."

Unknown

Feeding Time!

One of the benefits of traveling is that you develop friendships in many different places.

A friend of mine, who unfortunately has since passed away at a relatively young age, brought his family along on one of his business trips from Italy to the US.

We decided to take advantage of this opportunity for our families to meet and to get to know everyone better. So, we scheduled a barbeque and pool party at our home.

Luckily for us, the entire Italian family spoke English well, which reminds me of a joke one of my Italian friends told me:

"What do you call someone who speaks three languages? Trilingual.
What do you call someone who speaks two languages? Bilingual.
What do you call someone who speaks one language? American."

Unfortunately, a sad but quite frequently true statement. But I digress.

We decided to have a typical Midwest cookout menu of burgers and hot dogs on the grill, potato salad, coleslaw, corn on the cob, and strawberry shortcake.

After lots of playing and swimming, we all sat down to eat. Everyone seemed to enjoy the food, with the exception of the sweet corn. We figured out that none of our Italian friends even touched the corn on the cob. I didn't think much of it at the time, but it kind of nagged at me overnight.

The next day in the office I mentioned this to another colleague from Italy who had been in the US for a while. As I related the story, he chuckled and told me that Italians don't eat corn on the cob because it's considered to be "animal food."

In the Midwest, sweet corn was a summer highlight. But if the only corn on the cob you know about is raised for livestock feed, it is a different story!

"You learn a lot about someone when you share a meal together."

Anthony Bourdain

Danger in the Dark

I was based in Detroit but working for a company with headquarters in Phoenix. We had just gone through some significant reorganization with a new CEO and a new Senior Vice President of Sales and Marketing, the latter of which was my new boss.

An introductory meeting was scheduled in Chicago so as to be centrally located. My flight was at something like 6 am, so I was leaving home around 4:30 am. I figured that I would be nice and get dressed in the dark to minimize the risk of waking up my wife. Mission accomplished, I got dressed and left for the airport.

I got to the airport with no issues, boarded the plane, and flew to Chicago. Sitting on the rental car bus, I happened to glance down. What did I see – me with two different shoes on! Now, can it be two black or two brown shoes? Of course not, I had one of each.

Since it was a day trip to Chicago, I had no spare shoes. I tried to hide my feet under the bench, eventually got my rental car, and hit the road. There is no way I am meeting the Senior Vice President with two mismatched shoes, so the first thing I did was call one of my sales guys in Chicago and ask, "Where the heck can I buy a pair of shoes at 8 am?"

Luckily, it was a modest detour to that luxury retailer, Target, where I managed to find a pair of shoes that would get me through the day. The joke was likely on me as I've since been reminded that most men wouldn't notice if you wore the same clothes for three days in a row, let alone look at your feet. In any case, an embarrassing situation averted, though I was uncomfortable the entire day wearing $20 shoes that I was sure everyone noticed!

"Laugh loudly, laugh often, and most important, laugh at yourself."

Chelsea Handler

Amtrak Fiasco

Many years ago, when our boys were seven and nine, we had the great idea to take a train trip from Michigan to Colorado to go skiing for a week. We spent a lot of time (this is pre-Internet) researching our options and ended up booking the trip, travel and hotel, through Amtrak.

We chose to upgrade to large bedroom or family cabin accommodations, as available, for both legs of the trip. Our route was Ann Arbor, Michigan, to Chicago where we switched trains for the trip to Denver. In Denver we switched trains again to the Ski Train for the final leg to Winter Park, Colorado.

After spending the previous night at the ER with my younger son who had a horrible cough and fever, diagnosed as croup, we headed to the train station. Upon arrival we checked our luggage. It was a lot with four people and all our ski gear. We boarded the train to find that, while we had purchased first class tickets, there was no first-class seating on this particular train to Chicago.

As we walked through the train, we quickly figured out that there were no open seats at all, and people were sitting in the aisles. Bear in mind that this leg of the trip is five-and-a-half hours with multiple station stops.

A nice passenger noticed that we were traveling with a sick child and gave up his seat for us. So, we traded off who sat with one kid in the seat and who sat with the other on the suitcase in the aisle. Not a good start to our adventure.

We switched trains in Chicago and made our way to our room that had beds for all four of us and an in-cabin restroom. The design was clever, and the kids thought it was just wonderful. Once they figured out that they could walk between coaches, go to the snack bar, etc., they were having a great time.

As we were making our way to Denver, my wife decided to take a shower. We heard a yelp and figured out that the problem was ice cold water. I chased down an Amtrak employee in another car since our porter seemed to disappear right after boarding (and now we know why) and wasn't seen again until Denver.

We were informed that the hot water heater in our car wasn't working, so the water was basically at a temperature in the upper 30's since the water line ran on the outside of the car. I asked when it would be fixed, and he told me, "Not on this trip."

Later, we went to the dining car for dinner at our assigned time. After a considerable wait, we were seated and given very limited menus. We asked about the limited choices and were told that (1) they had some supply issues and (2) that not all the equipment in the kitchen was functional. Seems this was an ongoing problem on this specific train.

19

There were other issues that drove my wife and I crazy, but the kids still thought it was all wonderful. We transferred to the ski train in Denver and arrived in Winter Park a couple of hours later.

The week skiing was fantastic. We fell in love with Winter Park, the resort, the ski school, etc. In fact, we ended up buying a condo in Fraser two miles up the road from the resort later that summer and we kept it for many years.

Our kids made some friends in ski school, and we met up with them and their parents late in the week to ski and have lunch. While eating and having normal chit chat, the other father asked me what I did for work and how we got to Winter Park.

I launched into my detailed description of our Amtrak experience and how I dreaded the trip back home. I asked him what he did for a living, and he told me he was an Amtrak engineer. Talk about putting my foot in my mouth, but he wasn't surprised at all by my story (and he didn't hear the back half).

Our ski week came to an end, and it was time for the journey back to Michigan. We started out with a five-hour delay due to an avalanche between Vail and Winter Park. Can't blame Amtrak for that, but their station in Winter Park is small and it was not equipped to handle a bunch of people for an extra five hours.

We boarded the ski train for an uneventful trip back to Denver where we transferred to our train for Chicago. Our compartment was quite roomy with plenty of space to sleep four, but the bathrooms were shared in the middle of the car. Not a big deal, or so we believed.

We were about half an hour into the trip when they informed us that the bathrooms in our car were not functional, and we'd have to walk back one or two cars to use the bathrooms.

The next fun surprise was that we were informed the kitchen was completely non-functional. And the dining car was not open. We were told that they would bring us food for dinner that night and then breakfast in the morning.

I don't remember details of dinner, but believe it was something like pre-made sandwiches (i.e., they obviously knew of the issue for a while) and chips. Breakfast I remember well. We stopped at a railroad crossing in Ottumwa, Iowa (you know, the town where Radar O'Reilly of MASH was from). We were met by a pick-up truck that offloaded a bunch of boxes to the train. Breakfast was OJ, an apple, and a pre-packaged donut.

We eventually arrived in Chicago almost six hours late. We were told by the porter on the train that we missed our connection to Ann Arbor and would need to get a hotel for the night in Chicago.

So, we take our time before exiting the train as there is no rush, right? A baggage porter asked if we wanted help with our ample luggage and asked where we were going.

I said yes and asked him to take us out to where we could re-book and get a hotel, as we missed our connection. He asked us where we were going, and I told him Ann Arbor. He smiled and said, "See that train on the tracks next to us? That's the train to Ann Arbor."

He told us to follow him, and he proceeded to take us to the train without ever leaving the track area. We walked past the mass of people outside the doors waiting to board giving us dirty looks through the glass, got on the train, and stowed our luggage before getting seated. Needless to say, I gave the baggage porter a huge tip!

I was so upset with Amtrak that I wrote an incredibly detailed three-page letter outlining our experience. What bothered me the most wasn't the issues, but the absolute indifference of the staff (assuming you could even find them). No surprise, I never heard back from them.

It was over 25 years before I stepped foot on an Amtrak train again. It's too bad because train travel is great when done right as I've experienced in Europe and Japan on many occasions. In 2019 I had an opportunity to take the car train from Sanford (Orlando), Florida, to Lorton, Virginia (DC Area). I'll admit that while not perfect, it was a major improvement over my previous Amtrak experience, and I'd do it again.

"A certain combination of incompetence and indifference can cause almost as much suffering as the most acute malevolence."

Bruce Catton

Rocky Mountain Oysters

I grew up in a blue-collar neighborhood just north of Detroit. One of the clear memories I have of my early years is the food my mother cooked, and I'm being generous calling it food. Looking back, it is shocking to me that I ate it (guess I didn't know anything different at the time).

Meat was routinely cooked to the color and texture of shoe leather. In fact, one of our family jokes is that Mom would put the Christmas turkey in the oven on Thanksgiving to make sure it got done in time. As a result, my mother was very good at making gravy, since we had to re-hydrate the meat. To quote Irma Bombeck, "I come from a home where gravy is a beverage."

Also, it is worth noting, that I was well into my teens before I knew that vegetables other than iceberg lettuce did not grow in a can.

So, this was my culinary backdrop, where tuna noodle casserole was considered exotic, as I left home for college and beyond.

Fast forward a few years and I am a young engineer working for an electronics company. I have occasion to take a business trip to, of all places, one of my employer's factories in Ogallala, Nebraska. If you've never heard of Ogallala, you're not alone. To get there you fly to Denver and then drive three-plus hours northeast to literally the middle of nowhere –

or the middle of God's country depending on your perspective.

We conducted our business and headed out for dinner at the end of the day. I know now, but did not then, that my colleagues planned all along to have some fun at my expense that evening.

We got settled at the restaurant and the server, who knew everybody but me, brought us menus. I perused mine and my colleagues were not surprised when I asked, "What the heck are Rocky Mountain Oysters?"

They explained to me that they were the same thing as "bull fries."

"OK, but what's a bull fry?"

They gave me a look that only country folk can give to city folk and went on to explain that in areas where cattle ranching is prevalent, the young male animals are castrated. The resulting free testicles are skinned, pounded, and coated in flour, salt, and pepper and fried. They are generally served as an appetizer and also go by the names "prairie oysters" and "cowboy caviar".

They asked if I would like to try them, and I politely declined. They insisted they tasted like veal, but I just could not get past the visual.

However, all was not lost as during dinner I was regaled with jokes on the topic, two of which I still remember over 35 years later.

In the first story, a Frenchman is visiting Ogallala and goes to a restaurant for dinner. He sees an interesting dish go by and waves for the server. "What was that fried dish that you just delivered?"

She tells him that they are "bull fries."

Not knowing what that is, he asks for a description. She explains that they are bull testicles. Even being French, he is a bit shocked, and thanks her for the explanation. He continues reading the menu, suddenly jumps up, and heads for the exit.

The server yells, "Sir, is something wrong?"

He replies, "Yes, I just saw French fries on your menu!"

The second story, while not set in Ogallala, is still relevant. A businessman is on a trip to Spain where "bull fries" are known as "criadillas" or "huevos de toros" (bull's eggs). He is at a restaurant where he sees them being served in an un-pounded state. He asked about them and is told that after the bull fights, they castrate the animals and serve them in the restaurant. He is feeling rather brave and orders them. He thinks they are quite large and taste like high-quality veal. He likes them so much that he has them for dinner three days in a row. On the fourth day he orders them again. When the dish arrives, the "huevos de toros" are quite small.

He asks the server, "Why are these so small today?"

She shrugs and replies, "Sometimes the bull wins!"

"He was a bold man that first ate an oyster."

Jonathan Swift

WWF Encounter

In the late 80s/early 90s I was working for a European-based technology company. At the time, I was a sales manager based out of Detroit, and we were undergoing some significant organizational changes. As usual, some were good and some not so good. It was enough that it caused me to re-evaluate my position, confirm market value for my role, and decide whether or not I wanted to stay in my job.

I decided to fly to the US headquarters and meet with the executive management. Tending to "say what I mean" and "mean what I say," I basically walked into the vice president's office and said, "I quit."

This part of the story is not really interesting other than the fact that after a couple of days of talking and negotiating we decided that I would stay with the company along with a very significant pay raise. So, feeling rather proud of myself, I called Northwest Airlines and upgraded to first class for the trip back to Detroit.

The next morning, I headed to the airport early, noticed a minor commotion while checking in my rental car, and proceeded to the NWA agent to check in (yes, this is well before electronic check in was available). I asked him if he knew what was going on, and he said that a bunch of WWF stars were in the airport. I said, "Please tell me they aren't going to Detroit." He said, "Sorry, they are in fact going to Detroit."

A little bit bummed, I responded, "Let me guess, they are all in first class." Things got a little better when he replied, "Well, not all of them." So, I proceeded to the gate, where all was quiet, and I boarded the plane where I was seated in the last row of first class, seat A (window seat on left side.)

After a while, Jake the Snake boarded and was seated in the window seat opposite mine. Trust me, he was hard to miss based on his size and clothing. Next to board was the Ultimate Warrior, seated in the first row. A couple of others, who I did not recognize in street clothes, were seated in first class as well.

The door was about to close and the seat next to me was empty – yeah! Well, not quite. I looked up to see Andre the Giant crouched over and coming down the aisle. My first thought was – NO! Sure enough, he took the empty aisle seat next to me.

If you think airline seats today are tight, try sitting next to someone who is 7' 4" tall and weighs a bit over 500 pounds! My first thought was that if he yawned and stretched his arms, he would push me right out of the side of the plane.

I wasn't surprised, or unhappy, that he ignored me, but he was quite rude to the flight attendants. I spent the entire three-and-a-half-hour flight crunched against the wall of the plane barely able to eat my breakfast – and – so incredibly happy that I had spent my own money to upgrade!

Glad to have survived the trip and to be home, I was telling the story to my wife and kids, the younger of which was a major WWF fan at the time. Expecting, or maybe hoping, for some sympathy, what I got instead was my wife laughing and my younger son asking quite seriously, "So, did you get me any autographs?"

"Let the disappointments pass; let the laughter fill your glass."

Jackson Browne

Don't Pull a Thread

While I worked and lived in the Detroit area, my corporate offices for most of the 90s were in the Boston area. I was also raising kids at the time and tried to minimize time away from home. As such, I frequently took crack-of-dawn flights to Boston and did same-day returns when possible.

I was doing one of my same-day trips for a short notice and particularly important meeting. I got to the airport early, boarded the plane, and settled in for the relatively short flight to Boston. As I was sitting there, I noticed a string sticking out the seam of the inside right leg of my trousers. So, what did I do? I pulled it, of course. Could it have been a loose thread? No. The entire inside seam on the right side pulled out.

I had no spare clothes since I was doing a day trip, and there was no way to buy new suit pants. I borrowed some safety pins from a flight attendant and pinned things up the best I could to get me through the flight.

After getting my rental car, I headed for the closest K-Mart where I bought some thread and a needle. Sitting in the parking lot, I sewed up the seam the best I could to get through a few- hour meeting. Surprisingly, I managed to make it through without anyone being aware of the problem except me!

"Experience is a hard teacher. She gives the test first and the lessons afterwards."

Unknown

Yes, No Meat

When you work in the high-tech field, tradeshows account for a fair amount of your travel. This was the case the last fifteen years or so that I was working. While the shows require a lot of work both in preparing for the event and in actual attendance, they can be a lot of fun, too.

Germany was a frequent location for industry tradeshows; I went to Electonica in Munich, Embedded World in Nuremburg, and IBC in Amsterdam. After long days setting up, doing booth duty, and meeting with customers, we generally went out for a drink and dinner.

One night in Munich we decided to go out for an authentic German meal and some good beer. While this may not be light fare, it is certainly delicious!

It turned out that one of my colleagues, who we will call Jane to protect the innocent, was a vegetarian. After perusing the menu, she decided that a pasta dish would be the safest bet. So, when the waiter arrived, she explained to him that she was vegetarian and would like pasta with cheese sauce and no meat. He said, "No problem," took the rest of the orders, and went to the kitchen.

It was a busy time in the restaurant, so we enjoyed our beer and conversation while waiting for our food. When it arrived, the waiter proceeded to place a pasta dish in front of Jane that clearly had lots of chicken in it. She caught his attention and, pointing to the pasta, said, "This pasta has chicken on it," to which he replied, "Yes."

Jane looked confused and noted, "But I ordered it without meat." After a few seconds, his face lit up and he said quite earnestly, "Yes, no meat." At this point everyone except Jane burst out laughing.

While it is true that in America some vegetarians eat fish while others do not, that night we learned that at least to some Germans, if it was not beef or pork, it was not meat!

"I'm a secondhand vegetarian. Chickens eat seeds, I eat chickens."

Unknown

Beware of Hot Tubs

Sales meetings were a big thing in the 1980s and 1990s, and they often involved a fair amount of "acting out" that you normally didn't see at the office.

We were having one of these meetings in Phoenix where hotel rooms were reasonably priced, especially in the summer! Sales meetings were frequently "death by PowerPoint" (or more likely its predecessor, based on timing) product presentations and sales training sessions.

By the end of the day, attendees were bored and tired and ready to blow off some steam (aka drink a lot and get a little rowdy). So, after the group dinner one night, several people decided to go to the pool and hot tub.

Most likely due to consumption of too much alcohol, one of the attendees, we'll call him Fred for sake of the story, decided it would be a good idea to remove his clothes and get into a hot tub naked. A few of his "friends," and I use the term loosely, decided it would be funny to take his clothes and hide them.

That accomplished, they sat back to watch what would happen. When Fred went to grab his clothes, he figured out they were gone. I think his friends thought he would call out and start begging for someone to bring his clothes back.

"HAS ANYONE SEEN
MY CLOTHES?"

Instead, he stood up, walked from the hot tub and right into the lobby where he stood proud and stark naked and yelled, "Has anyone seen my clothes?"

I'm pretty sure we weren't invited back to that hotel, or maybe the company was too embarrassed, but we never had another meeting there.

"A man's true character comes out when he is drunk."

Charlie Chaplin

Eureka!

One summer when the kids were something like seven and ten years old, we decided to take a west coast vacation. We started with a few days in San Francisco and then drove the highway up the coast all the way to Seattle where we would visit some friends.

This is a great road trip with lots of scenery and smaller towns. You'll see everything from vast farming and cattle lands to the majestic redwoods to the rocky Oregon coast.

On our way up the coast to visit the Redwoods National and State Parks, we stopped for the night in the town of Eureka. We stayed at the Eureka Inn, an elegant historic hotel.

We checked in and relaxed a bit before heading down to dinner. We had a lovely meal and were enjoying the atmosphere, but the kids were getting restless after a day in the car. We talked it over and agreed that the kids could go back to the room, a short way down the hall, and we'd linger in the restaurant for a little while enjoying our glasses of wine.

Once finished, we headed back to our room. We had given the key to our kids, so we knocked on the door. Surprise! No answer. We knocked again, but louder, and still no answer.

Feeling the first pangs of worry, we yelled for the kids and banged on the door louder yet. By this time, people were coming out of their rooms to see what all the ruckus was about.

I ran to the desk and grabbed a hotel employee. I don't recall why, but she couldn't locate the extra key for the room. We continued knocking and yelling to no avail, worried that the kids hadn't returned to the room.

The hotel clerk located a maintenance guy who thought he had a way to look in the window of the room by hanging out of an adjoining room's window. He did this and said it looked like there was someone on the bed.

Now we at least knew they were in the room. While this was going on, the desk clerk returned with the spare key. We got the door opened. There were our two kids in bed and very sound asleep.

While we stood there relieved, but also quite humiliated and embarrassed, the kids slept through it all. We lost a few hairs through the process but managed to laugh about it a few years later.

"Good judgement is the result of experience and experience the result of bad judgement."

Mark Twain

Horse Sense

One memorable trip to Italy was centered on sales training. Just imagine a bunch of salespeople stuck in a conference room for days on end. Suffering again through death by PowerPoint.

One evening, our colleagues hosted dinner at an authentic Italian restaurant. One of the unique things at this restaurant was that the patrons were given aprons to wear that were, to say the least, a bit gaudy and silly, which helped to set the mood for the evening.

The food magically appeared at our tables, as did lots of great local wine. Salespeople, especially in the 80s, were known to imbibe occasionally and have a good time. On this occasion we lived up to our collective reputation!

One of my salespeople at the time, Libbie, was a horse person. She lived in the southern US, owned horses, and rode frequently. Since I was a graduate farrier (horseshoer) and horse owner, we had a lot in common. She, like everyone else, was feeling no pain when it was time for dessert.

We were shown various selections – tiramisu, various cakes and, new to Libbie, profiteroles. These profiteroles, which are a creampuff-type pastry with a custard filling, were dipped in chocolate and stacked in descending rows on a large platter.

Libbie asked the waiter what they were, and he told her in heavily accented English that they were profiteroles. She did not understand him, and he could not understand her either. After a couple of go-arounds, she pointed and tried a new tact, "Just give me a couple of those horse turds!"

While we do not think he understood, our crew did, and it was quite funny at the time.

Libbie has since passed away at far too young of an age, but I still think fondly of her and this evening out with friends.

"Here's to the nights we can't remember with the friends we can't forget."

Unknown

Secondhand Smoke

While I had done a fair amount of domestic travel, I set off on my first business trip to Europe in the fall of 1985. I was quite excited by the prospect of spending two weeks in Italy, a week in Milan, and then a week in Catania, Sicily.

I was flying from Detroit to Milan with a change of planes in London. I settled into my luxurious coach seat, ha. It was not that bad since in those days planes to Europe were generally half full, so you could move to a nearly empty row, and the seats were farther apart than today.

The flight from Detroit to London was about seven hours and was before the days of video screens, so I read quite a bit, ate what they called dinner, and tried unsuccessfully to sleep. We landed at London Heathrow, and I made my way to my connecting flight.

My next flight was on Alitalia. I went to the counter and handed over my travel documents. The agent asked if I wanted a smoking or non-smoking seat (yes, people used to smoke on airplanes). I asked for a non-smoking seat and was given a seat assignment in something like row 28.

Being an American, and only having flown US-based airlines, I was used to non-smoking being the first half or more rows of an airplane, with the smoking section being in the rear of the plane.

I said to the gate agent, "Excuse me, I asked for a non-smoking seat." She looked at my boarding pass and said, "Yes, that is a non-smoking seat." I replied, "But it is in row 28 in the back of the plane." To which she replied, "Yes, a non-smoking seat."

Getting a bit flustered I said, "But how can that be a non-smoking seat?" It turns out the plane was a DC-9. She thought for a minute, figured out the issue, and replied, "The non-smoking seats are the two on the left side of the plane and the smoking seats are the three on the right side of the plane." Kind of gives you an idea of how many Italians smoked at the time.

I looked at her for a minute before saying, "That is really dumb since the whole plane is then full of smoke." She had no reply to that, so I asked, "Why isn't the front of the plane non-smoking and the rear smoking so that the smoke stays in the back?" She thought for minute and said, "That could be an idea."

Obviously not something that anybody in charge had ever thought of . . .

"Don't spend time beating on a wall hoping to transform it into a door."

Coco Chanel

Fore!

Through the mid-80s and 90s, I worked in sales and sales management. We seemed to spend a lot of time in those days entertaining customers with lunch, dinner, golfing, etc.

This seemed to benefit the local engineering and purchasing community more than the people that worked in the factories. In fact, one customer engineer had a briefcase that he carried to the factory when visiting. It said "MEL," but the bottom segment of the "E" had fallen off. One of the people in the plant asked him, "What does that stand for, Mike's Free Lunch?"

On a trip to visit the customer's factory, I decided to take some of the people there golfing. As a result, I did something I had never done before. I carried my clubs and checked them as luggage.

We landed, headed to baggage claim, and stood around for about thirty minutes. An agent from Northwest Airlines came out and said, "Sorry folks, that is all of the luggage from your flight." I yelled, "Excuse me, but nothing has come out yet."

The agent got a worried look on his face and headed back into the luggage area. A few minutes later, coward that he was, he came over the intercom and said, "Sorry folks, it seems they never loaded the luggage in Detroit. Your bags will arrive tonight on the next flight."

My golf date with the customers was only an hour later, so off I went with no equipment. When I arrived at the golf course, I explained what happened and decided to see what I could rent.

They did have clubs for rent, so I took them, but not shoes. I had recently bought new golf shoes (that were somewhere in the air) and really didn't want to spend $60 on another pair of shoes, so I decided to golf in street shoes.

It wasn't like I was a good golfer to start with. In fact, when asked what my handicap was, I would normally reply, "my golf game." So, embarrassing shots were not an uncommon thing for me. However, nothing compares to teeing off with street shoes and spinning to the point that you almost fall down. I had more pulls and slices that day than you could imagine. Eventually, I figured out I needed to slow everything down and be happy with very short shots versus chasing balls two to three fairways away.

It was an embarrassing and humbling day, but the customers thought it was hilarious. They enjoyed retelling the story for many years.

"If your friends don't make fun of you, they're really not your friends."

Unknown

Menu Darts

When I was a novice European traveler, I found myself alone on a business trip to Milan. My hotel was downtown and upon checking in, I found that nobody spoke English. This was unusual in my experience, especially for an upscale hotel catering to international travelers. Unfortunately, I spoke zero Italian other than a dozen or so menu words. We struggled through as I gave them my passport and they figured out I had a reservation.

After dropping my luggage in the room, I headed out in search of a restaurant for dinner. I went past several restaurants and, having no other basis for comparison, picked one that was relatively full.

I held up my hand showing one finger and was shown to a table. A waiter appeared shortly thereafter and left me a menu. It was only in Italian and, upon asking, I figured out two things.

First, nobody in the restaurant but me spoke English. Second, they did not have an English version of the menu. I had apparently stumbled on a restaurant that primarily targeted locals and Italian travelers, which is generally a good thing.

No problem, I say to myself. Literally all the food I'd ever had in Italy was great. Feeling brave, I decided to play menu darts.

I closed my eyes, moved my finger around, and dropped it on the Antipasti section of the menu landing where it said *bresaola*.

Next, I moved to the Segundo Piatti section that I knew meant the main or meat dish. I skipped pasta as I figured I'd save room for dessert instead. Menu dart away I land on fegato di vitello al vino bianco e funghi. I had no idea what it meant other than white wine and mushrooms were included. Perfect. How bad could it be?

The waiter came to take my order and I pointed out my two choices, at which he broadly smiled, so I figured I'd done good. I also ordered *acqua minerale* and *vino rosso* (mineral water and red wine). My Italian vocabulary was growing by the minute!

The wine and water came, followed by the *bresaola*, an air dried, salted beef that was served with olive oil and parmesan. It was my first-time eating *bresaola*. It was outstanding and I was hooked for life!

After a suitable pause, my main course arrived. I must admit, it was one of the strangest looking dishes I've ever seen. The wine and mushroom sauce looked great, so I figured, what the heck, I'll give it a try.

It was like nothing I'd had before or since. It was very chewy and had a strange and rather strong metallic and gamey flavor. I was hungry and paying good money for the meal, so I choked down enough not to be embarrassed to leave the rest.

Because I wanted to get the taste out of my mouth and was still a bit hungry, I decided to go for dessert. Luckily, they wheeled a dessert cart over, and I was able to pick my dessert. I chose tiramisu that, with the red wine, did the trick!

The next day at the office I asked a colleague what the heck it was that I ate. He laughed and told me that I had ordered calf kidneys! Better that I learned that then, rather than while I was eating it.

The key takeaway from that experience for me was to make it a priority to learn enough of the local language to find your way around a menu!

"There is very thin line of demarcation between bravery and foolhardiness."

Anurag Shourie

Who Needs ID?

Anyone who travels a lot learns to adapt to cancellations, schedule changes, equipment changes, weather, etc.

I was flying from Detroit to Milan with a plane change in London. For our connecting flight there were mechanical issues with the plane, so we had a change of equipment.

Since it was a smaller plane, with a different seating configuration, everyone had to get new boarding passes. As we boarded, we figured out that besides different seating, overhead storage was almost non-existent and the space under seats was very limited.

As a result, many of us had to gate check our small bags as luggage. So, I grabbed my book out of my briefcase, handed my briefcase to the flight attendant, and settled in for the relatively short flight to Milan.

Upon landing, we exited the plane via the stairs, expecting to retrieve our gate checked items. At the bottom of the stairs, we were told that our bags would be available at baggage claim with the other luggage.

So, off we go to passport control and immigration. As we walked along, I saw a sign asking that you have your passport ready for inspection. It was at that moment that I realized that my passport, plane tickets, etc., were in my checked briefcase!

There were about ten people in front of me in line, so I had a few minutes to figure out what the heck I was going to say when I got to the counter. I decided to go with the truth, since that works best in pretty much all situations.

I stepped up to the counter and said, "I don't have my passport." The immigration official asks, "How did you get on the plane without your passport?" I explained that my passport was in my briefcase, and they made us check it after we boarded.

Surprisingly, he told me to proceed, get my bags, and then show my passport. Sounds easy, right?

I proceeded to the baggage claim area where I was surprised to see the *carabinieri* (the national gendarmerie of Italy) walking around with some sort of submachine gun held across their chests. There were also K9 officers sniffing luggage and people in all sorts of interesting places. All of this is a bit unnerving when you know you don't have a proper ID on your person.

When my bags finally came out, I quickly grabbed my passport and stuck it in my pocket. I then started off to figure out who I'm supposed to show it to. I couldn't go back to the original checkpoint, as that was marked as "Do Not Enter," so

I tried showing it to one of the officers. They were as confused, if not more, than I was.

Eventually I gave up and figured I was supposed to show my passport at customs when exiting baggage claim. I carried my bags over to the counter and had my passport and landing card in hand. The officer looked at my bags, grabbed the landing card, and waived me through without any care in the world about my passport because that had obviously already been checked.

I left the airport, got my rental car, and headed to the hotel. The hotel clerk asked for my passport, as usual, at check in. Curious, I asked him what they needed the passport for. He explained that they log guests in with the local police as they track visitors through the country. I'm thinking, great, they don't know I'm in Italy and they are going to log me in with the local police! Having no real choice, I handed over my passport.

The remainder of the trip went fine, and I got back to the airport for my flight home. As I approached customs at the airport, my thoughts were along the lines of, "What do I say when he can't find the entry stamp for Italy in my passport?" Turned out not to be an issue as he looked at the photo and quickly turned to an empty page and stamped it.

I'd pretty much put this out of my mind by the time that I was clearing customs in the US. I handed over my passport and a few moments later I was asked, "Where did you arrive from?" "Italy," I reply. "When did you arrive in Italy? I see an exit stamp, but where is your entry stamp?"

I was thinking, "Well do I have a story for you!" What I said was, "If there isn't a stamp, they must have forgotten when I landed in Milan." And there has never been another trip where my passport was out of my possession.

"Sometimes it's better to be lucky than good." ~ Spenser

Robert Parker

Departmental Clown

Early in my career I worked in the electronics division for one of the Big Three automakers. While our engineering offices were in the Detroit area, we had manufacturing plants in Toronto, Brazil, and Pennsylvania.

One of the job perks was a fleet of corporate aircraft that flew scheduled flights between Detroit and the plant in Pennsylvania. It made for an easy day trip with no airport hold ups, a dedicated and familiar flight crew, etc.

The morning flights out were somewhat subdued as everyone was focused on the workday that lay ahead. The return flights were more relaxed with food and drinks for the trip.

On one of our flights, one of our technicians, Roy, who was known as the department clown, was aboard. This plane was an older turbo prop and, while quite comfortable with sofas and large seats, the cabin pressure was not quite as good as the jets of the day.

As we were starting to make our descent, Roy, sitting near the rear of the plane, began experiencing significant ear pain due to the change in pressure. It got bad enough that he caught the attention of the flight attendant.

Roy was constantly joking around on these flights and the flight attendant(s) were the victim of several of his stunts. The flight attendant listened to him carefully as he described the issue.

She told him to sit still for a minute and she would be right back. When she returned, she had two red plastic drinking glasses in her hand. She very carefully explained to Roy that he needed to place one glass over each ear. She had a convincing story as to why this would work to relieve the pressure.

Roy did as he was instructed and placed the two red glasses over his ears. She told him it would only take a couple of minutes to start feeling some relief.

Meanwhile, she went back to the front of the plane, picked up the microphone, and announced over the PA system: "Hey everyone, look back at Roy."

Everyone looked back to see Roy sitting there holding red plastic glasses over his ears. Laughter broke out and, after turning a bit red, Roy laughed, too. In the process, his ears cleared!

Moral of the story: "Don't mess with flight attendants!"

"The art of medicine consists in amusing the patient while nature cures the disease."

Voltaire

Karma Is a Bitch

I worked for an Italian company for six years. As a result, I was in Italy two to three times per year for one or two weeks at a time. My visits were typically split between Northern Italy and Sicily, and I formed many friendships over the years.

I was based in Michigan and working with the Big Three. Our colleagues in Italy were designing the products that we supplied to our customers.

One of the things that I learned early on working with the Italians was that they could clearly and easily separate work and personal issues. In other words, they could have serious discussions (aka arguments) in a conference room, and after the meeting adjourned walk arm in arm down the hall talking about where they were going to dinner that weekend with their wives. As a young American, this was vastly different than what I experienced in the workplace, but I found it to be quite productive.

One of my colleagues, John, understood and enjoyed working in this atmosphere and was not shy to go head-to-head with some of our Italian colleagues. On one of our trips to Sicily, John had a particularly contentious discussion with Antonio regarding a design issue. Then, per Italian norm, all was good, and we went out to dinner with our Italian colleagues later that evening.

We went to a popular seafood restaurant in Catania. I was seated on one side of the table with one of our Italian colleagues, Antonio, to my right. John was seated across from me with another Italian colleague, Giulio.

Antonio asked John, "I'm going to have some *ricci di mare* as an appetizer. Would you please join me?" I suspected something was up and I was surprised when John, who did not want to back down from an obvious challenge, said, "Sure." I declined, as did Giulio, and Antonio placed the order.

Antonio tapped my leg under the table and nodded towards the other side of the table. I watched a restaurant worker several feet away put on some heavy rubber gloves, reach into a large fish tank, and pull out two sea urchins. This was all behind John, so he was clueless.

The guy proceeded to grab a nasty looking tool that he used to cut the sea urchins in half and then put them on plates. He then placed a plate in front of Antonio and the other in front of John.

If you have never seen a sea urchin like that, believe me when I say it looked rather disgusting. Antonio picked up a small spoon, dipped into the sea urchin, and took a bite of some yellow gooey stuff. John, not to be outdone, followed suit.

I could tell that John was not impressed by the texture or taste, but he held strong. As he went for bite two, he dropped his little spoon and stammered, "Its, its, its alive!" Sure enough, the sea urchin's spines were still moving around quite dramatically.

With friends like these, who needs anemones!

I must admit that I laughed so hard that I almost fell out of my chair!

"Revenge is a dish best served cold."

Proverb

Patience Is a Virtue

Because the Italian company I worked for had facilities in both Agrate (Milan) and Catania, Sicily, I went to both places often on business travel. On this particular trip three of us spent several days in Agrate and then flew down to Catania for a few days.

As we were leaving the office in Agrate, our Italian colleagues lined up. They shook our hands and said, "Thank you for visiting Italy, and we wish you a pleasant trip to North Africa." While said somewhat in jest, it seemed the north vs. south thing applied in many areas of the world!

While Sicily is indeed very different from Northern Italy, on my frequent trips I found the island to be very beautiful, the people as friendly as I'd come to expect of Italians, and the food, while more seafood-centric, quite delicious.

In Catania we stayed at our usual haunt, the Grand Hotel Baia Verde. The hotel is unique in that it is set on volcanic rocks overlooking a natural bay just outside of town. The rooms were quite large and comfortable, and it was an interesting place to go for a swim after a long day in the office, in a tiny cove surrounded by lava.

We conducted our business and after a week and half on the road were ready to finally head back home. After a nice breakfast, we set out for the airport in Catania. We dropped off our rental car, checked in, and then went to the gate for our flight to Frankfurt where we had a connecting flight to the US.

After boarding and waiting a while, an announcement came on that there was a mechanical problem with the plane, and we would be getting new equipment. We got off the plane and waited a couple of hours while they brought us a different plane. At this point we knew that we had missed our connection in Frankfurt, but there was a glimmer of hope for a later flight.

With the new plane, the boarding process was repeated, and we sat at the gate, again. The captain came on the PA and said, "We have a problem with one of the instruments. A mechanic is on the way and will fix the problem and then we'll be on our way to Frankfurt."

We saw the maintenance crew arrive and head to the cockpit. We waited and waited, and the captain finally came on and said, "The mechanic found the problem and needs to get parts. The repair will take a few hours, so everyone will please exit the airplane." Off we went again to wait in the boarding area.

Four or five hours later they figured out that there were no parts in Catania and that they needed to fly them in from another airport. At that point, they cancelled the flight and sent everyone to the service desk for flight and hotel arrangements.

This process took a couple of hours. I'm not sure what was going on in Catania that week, but there were no hotel rooms available in or near the city. They rebooked our flight for early the next morning and told us that our hotel was in Taormina. A minibus would be coming for us shortly to drive to the hotel. It was getting quite late by this point, everyone was tired, and an hour's drive to the hotel was not appealing.

Taormina is a beautiful resort town on the east coast of Sicily just up the road from Giardini Naxos. It sits at about 800 feet above sea level, and you can see both Mount Etna to the South and the Ionian Sea from the town. It has twisting medieval streets, a second-century Greek theater, and a cable car down to the beaches.

I had been there a few times before, and it was one of my favorite places to visit, so you can imagine how happy I was to arrive close to midnight and find that we were being picked up by a van at 5:00 am. No walking around seeing the sights or eating good food for us on this trip.

The hotel the airline put us in was quite nice. It had a very steep driveway down to the entrance where our driver deposited us. We checked in and, after the long day, went to our rooms for a short night's sleep.

We met in the lobby bright and early, well before breakfast was served, and waited for our van back to Catania. It arrived on time; we loaded our luggage and got in the van. The driver, for reasons I still do not quite understand, decided to back up the driveway rather than make a multi-point turn and pull out.

Most vehicles in Italy in those days had manual transmissions. The driver had difficulty reversing up the steep driveway and it took many attempts. On the fourth or fifth attempt, and with some pushing by us passengers, a lot of smoke was coming out from under the van, but he finally made it up the driveway and into the street. He got the van in gear, and we proceeded down the steep and winding road to the highway for the one-hour drive back to Catania.

Our first clue that something was wrong was when the driver had difficulty shifting. He managed to get on the highway, but he could not get the transmission to shift without a lot of grinding noise. It turned out he fried the clutch while backing up the hotel driveway, so he pulled the van over to the side of the road.

Luckily, one of my colleagues spoke Italian and was able to get the gist of the problem. The driver said that he would call his office in Catania and see what he was supposed to do. Of course, it was a little after 5:00 am, so there was nobody in his office. He told us we needed to wait a few minutes and he would try again.

After close to an hour with no success reaching anyone in Catania, he decided that he would walk and try to find a gas station or someplace where he might be able to get some help. So, he left us and our luggage in the van and started walking down the highway. We waited and waited and waited and there was no sign of the driver. While cell phones did exist at this time, it was well before any standardization, and you could not carry your US phone to Europe.

Our driver never returned, and to this day we don't know where he went. After waiting for close to two hours, we decided to ditch the van and walk back to a *pensione* (a cross between a small hotel and a bed and breakfast) that we had passed. Dragging our suitcases, we walked to the *pensione* and went inside. My colleague explained that we were stranded due to a broken vehicle and needed to get a driver to take us to Catania.

The nice woman at the desk made a couple of calls and told us that a car and driver would be there shortly. It was not urgent since, while we were having all this fun, our early morning flight to Frankfurt had left . . .

Our car and driver arrived not too much later. We loaded the luggage and set off for Catania again. The drive down was without any issues until we arrived in Catania Centro. We found downtown impassable due to a large accident. Our driver got out of the car and talked to some other drivers, some pedestrians, and a police officer. He returned to the car and told us the best way to get to the airport is to get out of the car here, walk a few blocks to get past the congestion, and grab a taxi.

Out we went, luggage in tow, and we started walking. Besides the noise, the fumes from all the small less-than-optimally-environmentally-controlled cars were quite obnoxious. Also, it was warm outside, so we were rough looking by the time we reached a taxi stand. It took only a few minutes, and we finally succeeded in getting a taxi to the airport. The car was quite small, and we went to the airport, in what was now late morning, with most of our luggage on our laps.

The Glamour of International Travel

We got to the check-in counter to find a flight and check our bags. As luck would have it, the next flight to Frankfurt was later in the day and would arrive after all flights to the US had departed. Resigned, hungry, and tired, we looked for someplace to eat and wait a few hours for our flight.

Believe it or not, the rest of the day went without incident. Our flight left on time, and we flew to Frankfurt. We collected our luggage and walked over to the airport Sheraton for dinner and a room for the night.

Morning arrived and here we were two full days into our journey. We got up, had breakfast, and headed over to the airport. Two of us were flying to Detroit, via Chicago, and the third was on a flight to Dallas.

We were feeling fairly optimistic and were flying on AA in business class. We settled in and, after boarding the rest of the plane, we took off. Something felt a bit funny on takeoff, but I could not really pin it down and the plane continued its ascent. A couple of minutes later the captain came on and told us more or less, "Well folks, you may have felt something on takeoff. We had a compressor failure on one of the engines and had to shut it down. This is a multi-engine aircraft, so it is not a major problem. However, we can't fly to Chicago without all of our engines in operating condition."

We were not given a reason for the failure and, based on what I later learned, I doubt that the flight crew knew the reason at the time. Airflow normally moves through a jet engine in a uniform manner. If something disrupts this flow, there is a chance that the compressor will stall. The most common reasons for this are bird strikes (as we hear in the news often), worn out compressor parts, and icing. It was a warm fall day, so we knew icing was not the problem. A compressor stall can result in a rapid, but short, loss of compressor performance or the entire loss of an engine.

The captain continued, "We need to return to Frankfurt, but we have too much fuel to land. So, we will be doing some large circles while we dump fuel and expect to land back in Frankfurt in about one-and-a-half hours." Seriously?

True to his word we landed back at Frankfurt airport about ninety minutes later. We were met at the gate by AA staff, as this was a full plane load of passengers that would need to be rerouted back to Chicago and/or their final destination.

Almost all the flights were completely full. Since we were business class passengers, we were pulled aside by the gate agent and told that they had secured seats for us on a Lufthansa flight to Chicago that was leaving in less than twenty minutes. Needless to say, we were relieved to be on a flight, but our luggage did not have time to make the plane change.

They loaded us on a golf-cart-type vehicle and took us to our connecting gate. We made it on time and proceeded to the jet way. They handed us boarding passes, we ran down to the plane, and they closed the door after we boarded. We looked around the business class section and, guess what, it was completely full!

We looked at our boarding passes, and it seemed they neglected to tell us that our Lufthansa ticket was in coach class. Not happy, we settled into our not-so-comfy seats for the almost eight-hour trip to Chicago. Other than tight seating and less than edible food, the balance of the flight was uneventful.

We landed in Chicago, experienced the thrill of clearing customs and immigration there, and headed to our connecting flight. After sixty-two hours of travel we landed in Detroit, walked out to our cars, and drove home. My luggage, however, arrived two days later . . .

I will admit that after this comedy of errors (one must try to take things in stride) I took future delays with much more patience and grace.

"When you have time to spare, go by air, otherwise take Greyhound!"

Joe Sczepanski, R.I.P.
(Friend and Co-Worker)

Outhouse? I Wish

My first overseas trip was to Italy in 1985. I very quickly fell in love with the history, historic buildings, and wonderful food. In fact, I loved the food so much that I gained eight pounds in two weeks!

Of particular interest to me was eating at restaurants that were frequented by the locals and not the tourists. The food and wine were always better, the prices cheaper, and the people friendlier.

We were eating dinner at one of these local restaurants one night. I needed to use the restroom and asked for directions to the *stanza de bagno*.

The waiter pointed to a door and said to exit and follow the path. Sounded a bit strange, but off I went. When I opened the door, I found myself outside.

There was indeed a stone path that I followed to a small stone outbuilding with a toilet sign on the door. I thought, "Oh great, an outhouse."

To my surprise, it was nice inside with lights and stalls with doors. I stepped into one of the stalls and froze. In front of me was not a toilet like I expected, but rather, for lack of a better description, a porcelain lined hole in the floor with a place for your feet on either side.

If all I needed to do was pee, I would have been fine. But I needed to do a number two, and I stood there looking at this "toilet" and wondering how could I do this and not fill my pants?

With some gymnastics (mental and physical) I figured it out, but I was gone from the table a while. My colleague and the waiter must have known I'd be surprised, as I was met with knowing smiles.

This was one of my early lessons in the value of learning as much as you can about other cultures and not making the silly assumption that everything is like it is at home. Like other potentially embarrassing situations, I came through it OK.

As it turned out, I found similar facilities, along with some standard-style toilets, in a couple of our other facilities in Italy. Many years later I also came across similar toilet arrangements while traveling in Japan and Asia. So, it's all what you're used to.

"Sometimes the most scenic roads in life are the detours you didn't mean to take."

Angela N. Blount

Oktoberfest

Visiting German Tier One automotive suppliers like Bosch, Siemens, etc., was a normal trip for me over the years. A colleague and I unexpectedly ended up in Germany in late September one time.

Since we were going to be there over the weekend, we decided to take advantage of our good fortune in timing and go to *Oktoberfest*. It was opening weekend and something neither of us had experienced before.

We took a combination of subway and taxi from our hotel and finally ended up at the fairgrounds for *Oktoberfest*. It was much larger and more crowded than anticipated with tents that were, in fact, permanent wooden structures.

Each brewery had their own tent which seated many hundreds, if not more, people each. So, we picked one of our favorite brews and headed into the tent.

It was absolutely packed with most attendees decked out in their *Oktoberfest* finest, lederhosen for the men and dirndl dresses for the women. The attendees dressed in the fashion of their home area, even those from outside Germany.

There was no walk-up bar service, and no empty seats at the tables, so we found our way to the back of the tent and stood by the wall. After being ignored by the waitstaff for quite a while, we got the attention of a server.

We looked very much like the typical American tourists in our jeans and shirts. She explained to us that you had to be seated to be served, and more importantly, needed a reservation to be seated.

A bit bummed, we made our way to the tent of choice number two. Same story. We quickly figured out that like all good Germans, they had their rules and intended to follow them.

Not being the type to give up, we wandered around outside looking for other options. Eventually, we found a beer hall where there were some tables outside with service.

Of course, they were all full. We watched as they rolled empty keg after empty keg out the back and set them up along the side of the building.

We had the bright idea to move one a few feet and make a table out of it. The servers were (and I apologize in advance for the generalization) all middle-aged women with large bosoms which they appeared to use to help carry eight or more large steins of beer at a time, a feat that I'm pretty sure I could not manage.

We caught the attention of one and raised two fingers. She gave us a funny look like "how did you crazy Americans manage that" and then walked away. A few minutes later our tenacity and creativity paid off when she showed up with a couple of beers.

We thanked and paid her and, after only three hours, enjoyed our first *Oktoberfest* beer!

Your Bier, Sir !

I have been back for *Oktoberfest* a few times since but with advanced planning and reservations compliments of friends and colleagues. What really impresses me about *Oktoberfest* is how it pulls the family and community together.

Entire families and big groups of neighbors attend together. Everyone from young kids to high-school aged kids, young adults, parents, and grandparents are all dressed in costume.

There is a litany of *Oktoberfest* songs and everyone (except some of the foreigners) know all the words. I've never experienced large-scale cultural events like this anyplace else, and it's stuck with me for all these years.

Bottom line is that if you are lucky enough to go to *Oktoberfest,* go with friends or co-workers who have reserved tables and buy, borrow, or rent proper *Oktoberfest* attire. You will not regret it!

"Success is stumbling from failure to failure with no loss of enthusiasm."

Winston S. Churchill

Beauty's Only Skin Deep

A customer, Joe, and I made a trip to Sicily on relatively short notice. Our normal hotel in Catania was booked, as was every other hotel within thirty miles of the city.

We ended up in a hotel near Siracusa, an interesting city in that it is rich in both Greek and Roman history and is the birthplace of Archimedes. I enjoyed seeing the sites there including the Greek Theater and the Ear of Dionysius

Upon arrival, the hotel looked nice from the outside and appeared to be from the nineteenth century. We entered the lobby and, though a bit tired, it was nicely furnished and decorated in period furniture.

Joe and I checked in and immediately went to the restaurant for dinner. As with all my trips to Italy, the food and wine was wonderful. At times I've wondered if it is a capital offense to serve bad food in Italy.

After dinner we retired to our rooms, as we'd had a long day traveling and needed to get an early start for the drive back to Catania.

When I walked into my room, I noticed a very musty and unpleasant odor. As I walked around, I found the room to be extremely worn, like carpet bare to the wood floor, and very dirty. Everything from the bed linens to the bathroom looked like they hadn't been cleaned since the place was built.

I knew there were not a lot of hotel options, so figured I just had bad luck. Rather than bother Joe, I decided I'd tough it out for the night and try to get a different room in the morning.

I quickly decided that there was no way I was sleeping in the bed. The bedspread was so dirty that I pulled it off and tossed it on the floor in the corner. I then got a couple of extra towels, surprised they were actually clean, and laid them on top of the blanket. I slept in my clothes on top of the towels.

When I got up in the morning, I went to give the bathroom a closer inspection. It was bad enough that I took a shower with my socks on and then threw them away!

I quickly packed and decided I'd go to the lobby to meet Joe and break the news that I wasn't spending another night in this hotel. As I walked into the lobby, there was Joe sitting on a sofa with his suitcase next to him. Turned out he had almost the identical experience to mine.

We checked out, and the desk clerk either didn't speak English, or pretended not to, as we explained why we were leaving. I'm pretty sure he understood as he gave a slight shrug and said "*ciao.*"

We laughed about it as our trip continued and ended up in the beautiful city of Taormina for the balance of our stay.

"A silk dress doesn't mean clean undergarments."

Proverb

Seal with a Pen

Security post 9/11 was a much different experience than what we were used to. Long lines and irritated/impatient travelers were a reality for a couple of years while TSA sorted things out.

I traveled routinely around the Midwest, frequently with colleagues. On one such trip, I was traveling with a colleague who had been in the military.

We were going through security, and the TSA pulled him aside to check his briefcase after it went through the X-ray. They pulled out a very small pair of fingernail clippers with a one-and-a-half-inch nail file on them.

They informed him that they would be confiscating the nail clippers. He discussed this with them a bit, but they held firm. Thinking he could convince them, he pulled out a roller ball pen and said, "I'm an ex-Navy Seal. There are eight ways I could kill somebody with this pen. Are you going to take it, too?"

The TSA agent very calmly said, "No, pens are OK." Our government at work busily taking care of us!

"Common sense is not so common."

Voltaire

Etiquette Be Damned

On one of our frequent trips to Germany, a colleague and I ended up in Munich. After leaving the office, we decided to head down to the *Marienplatz* to walk around a bit and grab some dinner.

The *Marienplatz,* which roughly translates to "St. Mary's Square," is the city's most famous square. It is located in the heart of the *Altstadt* (old town), and is full of historic buildings, shops, and restaurants.

As we started looking for a place to eat, we quickly figured out that everything was full and had long waits. While walking back towards the subway we passed a very nice restaurant that seemed to have a lot of open tables, so we went in.

We sat down and the waiter brought us menus. The food choices looked good, though a bit expensive, but that was OK since we were on the expense account.

After placing our order for a several-course meal, we noticed that there had to be at least a dozen pieces of silverware arranged around our plates. I grew up in a blue-collar area near Detroit and up to that point in my life I'd seen place settings with maybe four pieces of silverware, so this was a bit intimidating.

Our appetizers came and we grabbed a utensil and enjoyed the food. When they came to clear our dirty dishes, the waiter gave us a funny look, went away for a minute, and returned with some clean silverware. He proceeded to rearrange everything back to starting order, minus two pieces, and walked away.

The next course arrived, we grabbed utensils, and dug in. When they came to clear our dirty dishes this time, the waiter was less than amused. Again, he went away for a minute and returned with some clean silverware. He repeated his process of rearranging everything and walked away.

I thought this was getting quite amusing. Our main course arrived, I grabbed the wrong silverware, of course, and ate with gusto. Our waiter seemed to be genuinely getting perturbed as he went through his process a third time.

When dessert arrived, I started to get a bit frustrated, too. Here I was, a professional with an engineering degree, business experience, and a frequent traveler, and I could not seem to get the lousy silverware right. So, I raised my hands and said to the waiter, "I give up. Show me what silverware you want me to use."

Being an older German gentleman, I'm not sure if he thought it was funny or not!

"Sometimes you need a humbling experience to think about a few things."

Per Mertesacker

Parrot S*&t

Not having been to South America before, a good friend and co-worker and I decided to stop in Rio Di Janeiro on our way to Sao Paolo to visit a customer. We had a hotel that was across the street from the beach in Ipanema. It was summer back home in Michigan, so wintertime in Brazil, and the beach was quite empty.

We were tired from traveling and decided to relax in the room for a bit and check out Brazilian TV before dinner. We found a soccer game, and as I was a novice soccer coach for my son's pee-wee soccer team, we decided to watch it.

As we were sitting there, we kept hearing very loud noises, more like a roar, from outside every now and then. It took us a while, but we figured out that anytime something big happened in the soccer game, we heard the roar. It was the people around town watching and reacting to the game.

It turned out it was a World Cup qualifying game, and Brazil won. Before we knew it, there were thousands of people in the street celebrating. This was my first experience seeing the passion that South Americans have for soccer, since it was a relatively new sport on a broad basis in the US. I remember thinking that I'd hate to be here during the World Cup if they lost.

The next day we had time to sightsee, so we decided to explore Sugarloaf Mountain, the Christ the Redeemer Statue, and the Selaron Steps. We took the cable car ride up and the views were incredible.

We had a nice lunch and decided to walk around the area a bit before heading back to our hotel. As we were taking pictures, a guy walked up to my friend and placed a very large parrot on his shoulder for a photo opportunity. My friend was a trooper and went along with it.

I was snapping off some shots and broke into laughter. My friend asked, "What's so funny?" I responded, "It's not every day that you get to travel to Rio and watch a parrot s*&t on your friend!"

He replied, "Yeah, right." So, I said, "Look down at your left shoulder." Sure enough, there was a large amount of parrot poop down the side of his shirt.

Some trips are more memorable than others and I thought it was funnier than he did. I still have the photo over thirty years later . . .

"True friends are like loud farts. They don't smell as much, always make you laugh, and life is impossible to live without them."

Unknown

Huntsville Tornado

Huntsville, Alabama, was a frequent destination for me in the mid-to-late 1980s as my second largest customer had both design and manufacturing facilities there. On this particular trip we were meeting with some of the customer's purchasing executives, so my Vice President from Phoenix joined us on the visits.

It was mid-November, and as typical for the South, the weather was mild. This is an area where weather can change quickly and is prone to storms. In fact, I'd once stood in the back of the customer's old plant and watched a tornado move by several miles to the north.

We went to Huntsville on Tuesday, November 14, 1989, expecting Wednesday to be a day of thunderstorms. It didn't sound too ominous, and we were flying out Wednesday in the evening.

As we finished our meetings in the mid-afternoon, we were told that the weather was declining and that severe thunderstorm warnings and a tornado watch were in effect. Since we were on the southeast side of the city, we decided to get to our cars and head for the airport on the northwest side a bit earlier than planned.

While we were driving north up Memorial Parkway, with a separation between our two cars of one-half to three-quarters of a mile, a tornado warning was issued. In less than five minutes everything became surreal.

Suddenly it got quiet, and then it got dark. Next it truly sounded like a locomotive was going to drive through the car. It was over almost as fast as it started, and we couldn't believe what we saw.

Slightly to the north and off to my right, two square city blocks were basically gone! The devastation as we drove on was a bit unbelievable.

Turns out that a quick forming F4 tornado had just passed. That means wind speeds of 207 to 260 miles per hour, much more than a Category 5 hurricane. They estimated the tornado had a width of 800 meters max.

As I heard the news, I started doing some math. Our two cars, with me in the car furthest back, were about 1,000 to 1,300 meters apart and the tornado had a max width of 800 meters. Its path took it directly between our cars, so we had approximately 200 to 500 meters (less than 1,500 feet) to spare.

All I could think was what if one of us was going two miles per hour slower or we left the office one minute earlier? Miraculously the cars were completely untouched, and nobody was hurt, though we were a bit mentally shaken.

In the Huntsville area, twenty-one people were killed and several hundred were injured. Fortunately, everyone I knew in the Huntsville area was safe and uninjured.

We spent a couple of days in Huntsville waiting to get out, but in the grand scheme of things, a minor inconvenience. I've been in some dicey weather situations before, quick forming thunderstorms, large waves, and waterspouts, while boating on the Great Lakes, San Francisco Bay, and the Gulf of Mexico, but nothing compared to this. A couple hundred yards is all that separated us from disaster.

As they say, never underestimate Mother Nature.

"When you come out of the storm, you won't be the same person who walked in. That's what the storm is all about."

Haruki Mirakama

Starkbierfest

Germany was a frequent stop on my European travels. On one early spring trip, we were in Munich for a regional sales meeting. The group consisted of salespeople and applications engineers from Central Europe, and several of us from the US conducting the meeting and training.

Sales meetings and training can get boring after a while, so everyone looks forward to going out to dinner and having some fun. While Munich is well known for *Oktoberfest*, which is in late September, there is also another beer festival in the early spring between *Karnaval* and Easter. It is called the *Starkbierfest* (Strong Beer Festival) and runs for about three weeks.

I'll step back now and provide a short history lesson. In the 1600's some monks, the Paulaners, created the first *Starkbier* and it was named Salvator. While Stark means "strong" in German, and these beers do pack a punch, the name *Starkbier* actually refers to the amount of solids (or wort) in the beer. A liter of this beer contains the same amount of solids as a third of a loaf of bread. So, these beers were named *"Flussiges Brot",* or "liquid bread" and they were developed to help the monks survive the forty days of Lent.

The story we were told, which I am sure is half reality and half legend, goes like this. After developing *Starkbier*, the monks needed approval from their superiors to brew and drink it during Lent. So, they brewed a batch, filled up a barrel, put it on a cart, and took it to their superiors. During the trip, the beer spoiled. The beer was tasted, spit out, and their superiors told them, "If you want to drink this, go for it, but we'll pass," and the rest is history.

So, back to the *Starkbierfest*. Beer halls and breweries across the city of Munich host these festivals. The atmosphere is like *Oktoberfest* with thousands of visitors, many dressed in traditional Bavarian outfits. Rather than in the large tents of *Oktoberfest*, people pack into large beer halls, many at the local breweries. The beer is served in one-liter ceramic steins called *keferloher*. The patrons drink, sing, and dance on the tables and benches to both modern and old-time German hits. The funniest song, which was an every-half-hour event, has a chorus of "Who the F#*! is Elvis?"

Starkbiers are also high in alcohol content, averaging just under eight percent! So, while drinking it by the liter, and eating pork knuckles and spaetzle, you are pretty soon full, and you are feeling the effects of the beer.

Our main evening event was a trip to the *Starkbierfest* at *Paulaner am Nockherberg*, one of Munich's largest breweries that has been hosting *Starkbierfest* since 1870. There were about sixteen of us, so we took up an entire table. The first beers arrived quickly, and we ordered some food. The US contingent was warned by our German comrades to limit our consumption to one to two beers maximum. Recall, these are one-liter steins of eight percent alcohol beer!

Most of us behaved, but several had the "limit" of two because the taste is incredible, and it pairs well with the food. After a couple of hours of eating, drinking, and enjoying watching the Germans sing and dance, most of us were wearing down.

In Europe in general, and in Germany in particular, tipping was not a common occurrence in the 1990s. We had a particularly good server that evening. She interacted well with the group and was actively challenging one of our team members to drink another beer, which would be his third. He was hesitant, but she grabbed a full stein and downed about a half-liter in ten seconds. Not to be outdone, he got another beer and followed suit.

As we were preparing to pay and make our exit, we asked our server for the check. It was something around 300 euros, and since we had such a good time, a colleague and I decided to show her our appreciation and leave her a twenty-euro tip. That turned out to be a big mistake, as a couple of our German colleagues started yelling at us that it was Americans like us that were ruining the German economy, etc., etc. We were like, "What the heck are you talking about?"

Their concern, and despite liters of beer you could tell they were serious, was that the servers would be trained to expect tips! Rather than argue about it, we just laughed, which probably didn't help the situation, and we guided a few of our team out to the taxi stand for the ride back to our hotel.

AND 'GUTEN MORGAN' TO OUR AMERICAN SALES REPRESENTATIVES, WHO I BELIEVE HAVE ALREADY BEEN ENJOYING OUR GERMAN HOSPITALITY!

All were friends the next morning, having bonded over *Starkbier*. However, I felt sorry for the early morning presenters because it was midday before most were thinking clearly and able to concentrate!

"No good deed goes unpunished."

Oscar Wilde

Discover Zurich!

As can easily be related to today, flight delays, overbooking, and cancellations are the norm of plane travel. For most of my career, I was an Elite status flyer on Northwest/Delta and was generally taken care of when things happened.

However, I also had to fly airlines where I had no status. On one such trip to Europe, I had a lousy schedule home flying from Munich to Zurich to Chicago to Detroit.

All went well until we arrived in Zurich and were told that our plane had mechanical issues. The good news was they had found a replacement plane. The bad news was that it seated less passengers.

The airline asked for volunteers to take another flight. Maybe because it was Saturday and everybody wanted to get home, there were not enough volunteers to solve the problem.

My name was called, along with a couple of others, to go to the service desk. I walked over and was told that I'd been kicked off the flight. They used different words, but that was the gist.

It took a while, but they eventually got me booked on the Sunday flight, and because I pushed the issue, I got upgraded to business class. They also booked me a room at the nearby Hilton and provided food vouchers.

So, bummed that I was stuck for an unplanned day and night in Zurich and that I'd miss one of my son's soccer games, I headed to the hotel and checked in. I called home, explained what happened, and got the expected cool reception.

After grabbing a quick lunch in the hotel restaurant, I figured no harm in using my time to see Zurich, a city I hadn't been to before. The desk clerk explained the way to the train that would take me into the city. So, at about 1:30 pm I set off for town.

As I pulled in, the city looked quite interesting. I departed the train, it was now about 2:10 pm, and started walking. While walking by a store I noticed that the lights were out and there was a "Closed" sign in the window. What?

As I looked around, I quickly determined that everything in town closed at 2pm on Saturday and wasn't open at all on Sunday! Here I stood, stuck in Zurich, and nothing was open.

After walking around the downtown area and seeing the architecture, I headed back to the hotel to enjoy the "perks" of international travel, spending a day watching TV (not in English) and reading a book.

"When ill luck begins, it does not come in sprinkles, but in showers."

Mark Twain, Pudd'nhead Wilson

Penny Wise, Pound Foolish

For most of the 1990s we owned a condo in Winter Park, Colorado. While primarily intended for skiing, we found the area to be a wonderful place to visit in the summer as well.

We learned early on, the hard way of course, that my wife and youngest son were prone to altitude sickness. Turns out the best way to ensure it doesn't happen is to limit daily altitude changes to 5,000 feet, max.

So, it became our practice when going to Colorado to fly into Denver mid-afternoon and stay the night in a hotel. We then drove over the Berthoud Pass and up to Winter Park the next day.

On one such trip we were staying at an Embassy Suites Hotel in Denver. These hotels were characterized at the time by being built around a several-story-high courtyard.

In the middle of the night, I woke up to a sound that I couldn't quite place. I knew I was in a hotel and didn't understand through my grogginess why I thought I was hearing flowing water.

As I fully awoke, it was clear that I did indeed hear flowing water but didn't know why. I decided to get up and investigate and stepped off the bed into a couple of inches of very hot water!

It didn't take long to figure out that the source was the hot-water line feeding the bathroom sink that decided to break at 2 am. I quickly called the desk to report the issue. I'm pretty sure I woke the night clerk up, but he said something akin to, "Holy crap, there is water raining down from the fourth floor."

Sure enough, the water was flowing across our suite, under the door, across the hall, and then falling four stories like a waterfall.

Much to our surprise the front desk did not have access to the wrench required to turn off the water, as it was locked up by the maintenance team. I'm not sure how, but after a considerable delay, with water running through the hotel, the staff managed to get a maintenance guy onsite. He came up to our room and finally shut off the water.

We collected all our soggy stuff and were moved to another suite. It turned out to be a combination suite plus working room with a conference table and Murphy bed, but it was better than changing hotels.

Nothing like a little unplanned excitement for the evening.

"An ounce of prevention is worth a pound of cure."

Benjamin Franklin

Drunken Shrimp

When I traveled internationally, experiencing and learning about other cultures was a high priority for me. I tried to follow local customs whenever possible - wearing a yarmulke when eating in a Jewish home even though I'm not religious, walking around restaurants in my stocking feet or wearing a mask in Japan, wearing cartoonish aprons at some restaurants in Italy, etc.

Where I drew the line was the food that I ate, for example, no chicken feet in China and no raw or live fish and seafood in Japan. I grew up with grandparents who owned a marina, and raw or live fish is "bait" as far as I'm concerned.

I was a young quality engineer and was on a trip to Japan to visit a supplier with one of our senior buyers, Jerry. Since we were a big customer of the company we were visiting, and Jerry controlled the purse strings, several of their executives joined us for dinner.

One of the executives asked Jerry if he liked shrimp. Jerry proceeded to answer at length how much he liked shrimp. The executive told him he would order a special shrimp dish, *odori ebi*, or dancing or drunken shrimp, as part of his dinner.

Trust me when I say this is not a dish for the faint of heart. It's a form of sashimi and is basically live baby shrimp that are dipped in sake and then a dipping sauce before being eaten alive!

While Jerry would not have been surprised to see sushi on his plate, you could tell by his expression that he was not expecting live shrimp. Being brave, he listened as the customer explained how to eat it. Jerry ate enough to not embarrass himself, but it was clear he was not a fan. He admitted to me later that it was the worst thing he ever ate.

"OOH, PLEASE DON'T BE SO SHELLFISH!"

I had a similar experience at an "all lobster" restaurant. The first several courses went fine; everything was cooked. Then along came a beautiful dish with a lobster and flowers as the centerpiece.

It didn't take long to figure out that the flowers were stuffed where the tail meat used to be, and the tail meat was laid out nicely next to it sliced thin. Meanwhile, the lobster was still alive and moving its head and antennae. I politely declined to eat any because, "I can't eat something while it's watching me do it!"

So, while it is important to be respectful of other cultures, I learned how to politely say no. If it were internal company colleagues, I would simply tell them any raw or live seafood would have consequences! When it included customers, I would defer saying that I couldn't eat fish or seafood.

"Food is not rational. Food is culture, habit, craving, and identity."

Jonathan Safran Foer

Fashion Forward

In the early 1990s I had an opportunity to take a week-long sales management class in New York through the American Management Association. This was at a time when "business casual" was just starting to become a reality with just "business casual Friday," if at all.

With that in mind, and the fact that sitting in a classroom for a week wearing a full business suit just sounded stupid to me, I made it a point to read the course description. While doing so, I saw in bold print the words "casual attire." Since I'm a guy that hates (probably not a strong enough word) suits and ties and thinks that dressing up for dinner is putting on a clean t-shirt, I was very happy.

So, I carefully packed khakis, golf shirts, etc., for my trip, refusing to pack anything remotely formal. My wife, who was more conservative than me, was a bit suspicious as this was kind of radical at the time.

I arrived in New York and checked into my hotel for the night. The next morning, I walked over to class excited for the week ahead.

Not long after I took my seat other people started walking in. Being the observant guy that I am, I quickly noticed that the men were wearing suits and the women dresses or pants suits. I thought to myself, "Can't anybody read?"

The classroom filled up and the instructor walked in, and he was wearing a suit, too. He looked around the room and then his stare landed on me. Not one to be easily embarrassed, especially when I thought I was right, I looked around, back at the instructor, and said, "Well, at least one of us will be comfortable this week." He apparently didn't know how to respond to that, so he said nothing.

That's not what I meant by 'leisure wear'.

Turns out that the class description, I checked when I got back to the hotel, did indeed say casual attire, but was preceded by something like "dress code is business attire except for classes held in resort locations where it is casual attire." Oops!

Since it was summer and hot, most people were clearly uncomfortable in the room. I think it was day three when the instructor said, "I think Harvey had the right idea. Feel free to come in business casual clothing if you want to for the balance of the week." Ha, redemption!

I like to believe that I had a small part in pushing the move to business casual forward. By the time I retired less than twenty years later, business casual was every day and jeans on Friday (if not more frequently) in my industry!

"Follow your own path no matter what people say."

Karl Marx

Rental Car Swap

While working in sales and marketing roles, traveling was a normal part of the routine. I found it interesting that most people I knew and met thought I was lucky to get to travel as much as I did. Little did they know . . .

Early on there may have been a little truth in that. However, as most road warriors will tell you, travel is exhausting and frequently boring. The reality is that a hotel room is by and large a hotel room, conference rooms look pretty much the same around the world, and bad room service is frequently the norm.

I recall a trip where, upon landing, I headed to the car rental counter. As usual they didn't have the type of car I had reserved, but this time they actually had an upgrade for me.

So here I was, in my twenties, driving out of the rental lot in my new burgundy Cadillac Coupe de Ville. Not being able to find your rental in parking lots was common, so I figured I was all set with this one.

I drove to the customer's site, conducted our meetings, and then headed out to lunch with one of my customers. We arrived at the restaurant and left the car with the valet for parking.

We had a great meal and conversation and then went to the valet to retrieve my car. I gave him the ticket and told him it was a burgundy Coupe de Ville. He smiled and said he knew right where it was.

He brought the car, my customer and I climbed in, and we drove fifteen minutes back to the office. Upon parking, I reached behind the back seat to get my briefcase, but there was nothing there.

I asked my customer if he remembered seeing my briefcase, and he said yes, he remembers I had it when we left the office. Upon further investigation, I noticed a jacket and other things on the back seat that weren't mine either. I looked at the keys and, guess what, no rental car tag!

Apparently, the valet had given me somebody else's car. What are the odds of there being two burgundy Coupe de Villes at the same restaurant?

At this point I was freaking out because not only was I driving the wrong car, but my briefcase was in the other car. I pictured the owner of this vehicle driving away from the restaurant not realizing he had the wrong car either. A timeline appeared in my head where I would miss my flight back home.

I climbed in the car and drove back to the restaurant. When I jumped out of the car, the valet saw me and looked confused.

"You gave me the wrong car." He looked at me and all color drained from his face. He took off and quickly returned looking somewhat relieved. My car was still there!

I gave him the keys and he re-parked the car. He then came back with my rental. I think he was afraid that I was going to make a big deal out of it. He was relieved when I said, "I won't tell anybody if you don't!"

Luckily this was the first and only time that something like this happened to me.

"It's not who was right or who was wrong when a mistake was made. It's about who learned from it."

Robert Kiyosaki

Flying Crabs

Since we both worked full-time, my wife and I put in extra effort to spend as much time with the kids as we could. We put a lot of work into planning multiple vacations every year that offered a variety of experiences; skiing, outdoor adventures, theater, museums, history, etc.

When the kids were around eight and eleven, we took a trip to Washington, DC, and the Chesapeake Bay area. Besides all of the normal DC attractions, we went to Colonial Williamsburg, Six Flags, and Tangier Island.

Without going into too much detail, Tangier Island, Virginia, was settled in the late seventeenth century. The original settlers farmed but were always watermen dependent on harvesting crabs and oysters, which is now their primary occupation besides tourism. They speak a unique dialect of English that evolved due to their isolation from the mainland and is very difficult for others to understand.

After exploring the island, we decided to go to one of the restaurants and eat some crab. Even though the restaurant was quite full, we were able to get a table.

While we were perusing the menu, which was primarily crab as expected, my younger son noticed people at other tables hitting the crabs with a hammer. We asked a server about this, and she explained how you cracked the crabs using a hammer instead of the plier-type tool we were used to.

Three of us, including my younger son, ordered a large platter of crabs. Our older son, not liking shellfish, ordered something off the landlubber side of the menu.

Our food arrived and the crabs looked great. My son grabbed a crab, put it on his plate, and raised his hammer. Before we could say anything, he took a swing.

While he did make contact with the crab, it was a bit indirect, and the crab went in the air. It landed on a table about ten feet away, and it shocked the woman sitting there.

We were horrified and trying not to laugh at the same time. She turned and saw this cute eight-year-old, clearly excited about cracking crabs with a hammer and then eating them, looking at her and still trying to figure out exactly what happened. Thankfully she smiled and said something like, "It could happen to anyone."

Potential crisis avoided, we proceeded to enjoy our lunch. Afterward, my son went into the gift shop, showed me a souvenir hammer, and mentioned that he wanted one. Figuring it was a good memory, I bought it. Thirty years later and it's still in a box in my son's storeroom.

"Did I do that?"

Steve Urkel
Family Matters TV Show

Nice Try, Dad

One of the perks of flying a lot is accumulating miles that can be used for free travel. Granted it was easier to do that thirty years ago than it is now. Our family took many trips using my miles. I've earned about 3.5 million credited flight miles to date, and we traveled to Europe, Hawaii, and around the continental United States on those miles.

When our kids were four and seven, we planned a trip to Hawaii. Since the thought of having built-in babysitters was attractive, we offered to fly my parents over with free airfare and hotel, which was an offer they couldn't refuse. They had never been to Hawaii.

We flew straight to Maui but flew my parents to Oahu first so that my dad could go to Pearl Harbor. They caught up with us a couple of days later and joined us in the large waterfront condo that we had rented for the trip.

One day we were in the Kaanapali/Kapalua area sightseeing and shopping when my dad ran into the store we were in and said, "I want to go parasailing." While my dad liked to have a good time, this was a bit of a stretch considering he came close to drowning a couple of days earlier while snorkeling.

My dad was in his mid-fifties at this time and had been known to tell younger women, including my now wife when I started dating her, "If I was only twenty years younger." My mother just stared at him while my wife and I were like, "Huh?" A couple of minutes later a tall, beautiful young lady wearing a teeny bikini walked into the store and waved at my dad. Guess what, she was the parasailing instructor!

My mother quickly figured out what he was up to and walked over to the young lady. She quite loudly asked if she and her seven-year-old grandson could come on the boat, too. My dad, who was only 5' 9" tall and 140 pounds, managed to deflate when she answered, "Yes, by all means please do."

So, while he did get to go parasailing, he had to do it under the watchful eye of his wife and my continuously questioning son. Not quite what he had in mind, and it probably didn't help that I laughed my ass off!

"Curses! Foiled again!"

Dudley Do-Right
The Rocky and Bullwinkle Show

Lady Sings the Blues

My wife and I went to Chicago for a long weekend with some good friends, Scott and Debbie. While we had been to Chicago several times, it was Scott and Debbie's first trip there. We did a lot of sightseeing including the Miracle Mile, Grant Park, and an architectural river cruise.

No trip to Chicago is complete, in my opinion, without hitting a few places to hear live blues music. On Sunday, we decided to hit a few of my favorite spots. The plan was that we would go to Buddy Guy's Legends first since it was a bit more touristy and would get crowded earlier. After that we would hit Clark Street and go to Chicago Blue and Blue Chicago.

Even in the late-afternoon Buddy Guy's was crowded, and we ended up at the stand-up tables towards the back. We figured we'd have a drink, listen to some music, and then move on. You never knew what to expect here, and, if you were lucky, "Buddy was in the house." That had only happened to me once before, so we weren't overly optimistic. I've taken many people to Legends who claimed to not be "fans" of the blues. I'll assert that anyone who has ever seen Buddy Guy perform live, especially in a small setting like his club, will be transformed into a fan of both Buddy Guy and the blues! That is exactly what happened to me on one of my first business trips to Chicago.

Fate was on our side that Sunday, and the announcement came over the PA that Buddy was in the house and wanted to say a few words. He walked on stage to much applause and proceeded to talk about his good friend and blues legend Koko Taylor. He said that today, which was September 28, 2003, was her seventy-fifth birthday. He wanted to celebrate.

In case you're not a blues fan, Koko Taylor is frequently referred to as The Queen of the Blues, and she had a career spanning forty-five years. The shock came next when Buddy told everyone that Koko Taylor was "in the house," and that he was going to have a birthday party for her. And we were all invited to stay for the festivities!

Buddy kicked off the party by introducing Koko Taylor to the crowd. He remained on stage and played a few songs, followed by a seemingly endless string of blues musicians that came for the party and took the stage for a song or two. Somewhere in the few hours of the party the entire house sang Happy Birthday to Koko. The highlight of the night was Koko Taylor performing a few of her classic songs and her teenage granddaughter taking the stage and singing with her.

We stayed for the entire event, and we never made our way to Clark Street. When you travel a lot, you learn to go with the flow, which in most cases means dealing with unforeseen problems. This was one of those rare times that Lady Luck smiled on us.

We traveled with Scott and his family many times over a ten-year period. Unfortunately, Scott died a few years later at too young of an age. When I think of Scott, which is often, this trip always pops into my head as a truly special evening spent with special friends.

"I've found that luck is quite predictable. If you want more luck, take more chances. Be more active. Show up more often."

Brian Tracy

Safe Travels

Buen Viaje

Bon Voyage

Yoi Tabi Wo

Turas Maith

Boa Viagem

Buon Viaggio

Schöne Reise

ACKNOWLEDGMENTS

My wife, Alina, has been an invaluable resource in organizing and editing this book as well as providing me support and encouragement along the way. My English Cream Golden Retriever, Smoky, serves as my Chief Morale Officer and kept me company while I was working at the computer. My illustrator, Guy Harvey, created brilliant artwork that tied everything together and put the finishing touches on the stories. My copy editor and proofreader, Adria Carey Perez, cleaned up my many structural and grammatical errors; I am an engineer after all, and my writing is better for it.

Smoky – Chief Morale Officer

ABOUT THE AUTHOR

Harvey Steele retired from the high-tech industry after more than thirty years working in various engineering, sales, marketing, business unit and general management roles. He lives in Minnesota with his wife Alina and English Cream Golden Retriever Smoky. He enjoys spending time with his family, especially his two grandsons, traveling, blacksmithing, jewelry design and fabrication, glassblowing, and writing.